I0415310

MIXED EMOTIONS

Dedications

To my family and to you the readers. I hope that you enjoy reading and thank you for your purchase.
-Lynn

Chapter 1:

The door opens on the third floor and the girl with the bright cherry gloss lip stick and big hair walks out the elevator. I don't know her name and have never even spoke to her but I see her every morning. We ride three floors together and every morning for those three floors I wonder what possess her to wear that bright red ass lipstick. Good thing she works inside the building and not outside. I adjust my skirt and take a quick look into my compact, just to make sure my face is straight because I know who walks through the elevator doors on the next floor. Though I don't know him I have had wild crazy passionate sex with him in my dreams several times. I don't talk to him either. I just ride my several floors in silence. "Ding". The doors open. Well damn, there he is looking exceptionally good today. Smooth creamy chocolate skin tone, fresh low hair cut edged up nicely with waves that would make you sea sick. He is so damn fine and dresses nice all the time. He only stands about five feet five inches which is kind of short for my taste but that's alright cause judging by the size of his feet, I could tell he was packing. He always gave me that look like "Don't let the height fool you". Uhhhmm look at them lips. He has the sexiest lips I have ever seen. Nice and full, and he was always licking them. I bet he could eat the hell out of some pussy. As he got on the elevator I tried to act as if I didn't see him and I was also trying to act like I wasn't picturing him walking over to me and throwing my body against the wall and having his way with me. Every morning it's the same thing. Every morning I want to speak but something clogs my throat and I end up just standing there looking dumb, which is not like me at all. Normally when I see something I want I go get it. I'm never shy always outgoing. But there was just something about him that made me just stare in amazement.

He looked so mean. So rough yet he always had on a nice button down with slacks and what look like Stacy Adams. Maybe tomorrow. I'll speak then, yeah tomorrow.

As I get off the elevator and walk down the hall I think about Daddy. Secretly that's what I called him 'cause he looks like he takes charge, like he puts it down. But let me push that to the left. Time to get to the money.

I work for Larson's Telemarketing Company so I spend hours on the phone. I have my own little cubical just like everyone in here. My job is to try to get people to buy timeshares throughout the U.S. For every one that I sell I get one hundred and fifty dollars extra on my check. No, my hourly pay isn't much but I make up for it on my commission. I don't let a day go by that I don't sell at least three. And that's how

I stay fly. Hell I'm twenty-three years old, I live by myself and I'm pushing a 2011 midnight blue Range Rover. I'm one of those independent women they sing about in the songs.

My job is on the 6th floor of our building and it's the only office on this floor. But on the fourth floor there are two offices, some car loan place and an insurance office. I'm not sure which one Daddy works in but he looks like it might be the car loan place. And damn do I want a loan.

The hours went by pretty fast today with me selling four timeshares. Today was a great day. Usually on nights like this I treat myself and hit the club with my girls. This is just what I decided to do. So I called them up.

I got everybody's voice mail so I left them messages.

"Hey girl it's Desi, you know its Friday and you know I want to hit the club tonight so hit me back alright. If you don't come I'm rolling solo. Either way I'm partying tonight. Call Trae and I'll call Diamond. Call me back girl, Bye".

As I'm in the elevator on my way to my car my phone goes off.

"Hello"?

Damn it's that guy I met at the club last weekend. Why did I give him my real number? He is such a bug a boo. He has called me every day this week. And it's always the same thing when am I going to let him get in these drawls.

"How you doing sexy? Did you me miss me"?

"I just talked to you yesterday I didn't have time to miss you. What up though"?

I think that was kind of rude. Possibly, but who cares I'm ready to drop this one for real.

"Just trying to take your sexy ass out so I can drop it in your drawls, you know".

I'm bout to let his ass know now.

"Listen I gave you my number because I thought you were cute but now that you have called me three times a day everyday this week I can see that you are pretty damn annoying. And for the record *let me drop it in your drawls* is not cute damn't. Loose my number K. BYE."

Hopefully his ass gets the picture now

but knowing him he'll be calling me tomorrow. I got in my car and the radio was still bumping loud from this morning and all I heard was

"I get so weak in my knees I can hardly speak, I loose all control and something takes over me"

damn and that's how I feel when I see Daddy. I drove home wondering how he felt about me. Wondering if he thought about me on his way home as well. Was he just as intrigued by me as I was of him? Did he have a girl or wife or kids? He looked like a bachelor. I could picture walking in his house. I pictured him living in a loft somewhere downtown. With black and chrome furniture. I pictured him having nothing but imported water and wine in his refrigerator. And him always eating out. I pictured him having a king size bed that I always laid in as he would slide his tongue all over my body. I could imagine him driving a Lexus on some 20's or something like that. And I bet he listens to H-town and Jodeci. As I pulled into my parking spot I could feel myself get moist. I knew I needed to take a shower so it was fine with me because my double headed shower head would come in handy. I walked through the door and placed my keys on the table and kicked off my shoes. I pressed the answering machine button to check my messages and there was only one. It was dumb ass from the club.

"Hey girl, I just wanted you to know that I ain't mad at you, I love it when a women takes charge like you. And I can't wait to see you again. Alright then gone".

Ugh. He was not going to spoil my mood. I made nice money today, I'm bout to hit the club, and I could feel myself moisten up from the visions of Daddy again. I lay on my bed and reached into the third drawer on my nightstand and pulled out my man. My man was smooth. He was about 12 inches long. He had beads that swirled around his shaft and bunny ears connected to his base. He had become my best friend lately. Men these days just weren't stepping up their game. I laid my head back and closed my eyes. While my man was on low speed I let my mind drift back into Daddy's loft. Lying on his couch. I saw him kissing my neck, (*yes*), I felt his tongue lick the bottom of my ear lobe and roll down my neck. The beads continued to swirl. I saw him rip his shirt off and lay on top of me. I could vision his thick hard love slide in me so did my man. Everything he did my man did and with every moan I made, my hips would rotate. With every stroke he gave me my man would glide in and out. As I clawed

Daddy's back my man's speed increased. It was no longer at a low speed it was now going full throttle. I could feel my body begin to shake and I knew what was going to come next. That point where I could hear nothing. I could see nothing. My body would begin to shiver and as I felt it drip out onto my bed my man's beads slowed to a stop. And all I could do was lye there motionless and satisfied. And for 30 minutes that's just how I stayed. Finally I got up and went into the bathroom and took a shower. With every pound of the water my body felt great. After about 20 minutes I got out the shower and threw my sheets in the washing machine.

The shirt that I picked out hung over my shoulder perfectly so that my cheetah print tattoo that went from the front of my shoulder to my back showed completely. The men were going to be on me tonight.

Chapter 2

My phone started ringing and I answered it.

"Hey Trae what's up,"

She sounded like she was crying.

"Desi, Desi can you come get me please. This boy tripping because I caught him cheating, in our bed, Desi, our bed. I jumped in and beat that bitches ass and now he mad at me. I got to get out of here can you please come and get me".

Just hearing her cry I was already in my car, and on the way.

"What the hell I'm on my way, don't even trip. And tell him and that bitch they better not be there when I get there".

Trae didn't live that far from me it was about a 10 minute drive. So I knew I would be there in no time. I called

Diamond and told her to meet me there just in case some shit pop off. By the time I got there Trae was throwing his shit in the front yard and pouring bleach on it. The bitch was gone but his ass was still there trying to call the police or something. I grabbed Trae and told her to grab her things.

"Girl lets go, fuck this clown you ain't got to take that shit. Get your stuff you can come stay with me for a while."

With tear filled eye's she grabbed her things and we left. Diamond never did show up. She called back though.

We got back to the house and settled in I no longer felt like hitting the club I just wanted to lay it down and relax with my friend. I climbed in the bed and Trae climbed in next to me and laid her head on my shoulder and we fell asleep.

Chapter 3

I saw the cherry lipstick girl on the elevator again this morning, it never fails. She gets on and exits on the same stops every time. Then she gets off with out saying anything to me just staring at me yet another morning. I fix my clothes and take a quick look in my compact. The Elevator doors close and open quickly and as she exits in walks Daddy, once again looking fine as ever. And yet once again I can't work up the courage to say anything. He glances my way and smiles at me. *Speak damn't.* But I didn't have to because he did.

"What's up with you"?

BOOM! The elevator shook real hard and stopped. I screamed.

"It's stuck".

I fell against the wall and Daddy ran up to me and grabbed me.

"Are you OK"

He asked as he held me tightly. Damn he smelled good.

"Yeah, I'm good".

My body slid down the wall and I sat on the floor. I looked at him and said

"can you please push that red button so we can get some help"

as he stood up he said

"what's the rush maybe we can talk for awhile. I mean, I see you everyday and you don't even look at me".

In my mind I'm thinking oh, I be looking at you. I just smiled and said

"I have to start work soon."

"Talking to me and giving me your number is not going to make you late for work, by the way I'm Stacy."

"How you know I want to give you my number"?

"You do. So how bout it".

He just proved me right about the name I gave him. Daddy, taking charge already. So you know I gave him my number right? I wrote it down on a piece of paper that I had in my purse and he helped me up. As I went over to the wall so I could push the red button, he said I'll get that for you. And he hit the button.

"Hello, we know you're stuck and help is on the way. Just hang in there for a few more minutes. Is anyone hurt? And how many people are in there"?

"There are only 2 of us in here and no one is hurt."

"Alright, hang in there."

I am so not going to miss work for this but then again, hell yeah I'm in the elevator with Daddy. This is like a dream come true, for me anyway. I wonder if this is a dream come true for him too. Damn he looks good. Even though was he standing on the other side of the elevator I could smell his scent all over me. And just smelling his scent makes me want to melt right here. The buzzer rings on the elevator and the lady begins to speak.

"It's going to be about 30 min before anyone can get up here to fix the problem. It seems the elevator is stuck between two floors and the only one who can fix that is the supervisor. I will keep you posted".

30 min, damn I'm going to be late as hell and to top it off my phone don't get reception in here.

"OK" Daddy responded. And he walked over to where I was sitting, and then sat down beside me. My whole body started tingling. I didn't want to seem nervous so I tried my best to calm down.

"All this room in here and this is where you want to sit"?

"Hey why not it's a great seat. Do you know what a better one is"?

I could think of one but what is he talking about.

"No I don't, why don't you tell me"

but he didn't say anything he just placed both hands on his lap in a patting motion. And I was shocked because he never said anything to me and I always wanted him to. I just smiled and shook my head

"you a mess".

He rubbed his legs and said

"OK but it's the best seat in the house"

and he started laughing. I never had a chance to see it but he has the prettiest smile I have ever seen. With him still sitting on the floor and his back against the wall I stood up and stood over him. I didn't know what came over me but I just had to see what he would do since he was talking all of that shit bout it being the best seat in the house. I had on a skirt and with the way I was standing over him I knew he could see right up it. He placed his hands at my ankles and rubbed my legs. His hands moved up the length of my legs till they were under my skirt. He had the softest hands I had ever felt. They seemed to just glide up my legs and into my panties. And I could see his eyes get wide when he felt how wet I was. His finger slid into my body with ease and I could feel my walls tighten around it. As he pulled his finger out my juices dripped out and he pulled me closer while sliding down my panties. Please don't let them fix this elevator no time soon. As he took my freshly shaved pussy into his mouth I moaned a soft whisper of *YES*. Still sitting on the floor his tongue slid in and out of my body. With my hands and my face pressed against the wall my legs began to shake and tremble and I tried to walk away but I couldn't cause he tightened the grip on my legs pulling me closer and taking more of me into his mouth. As my juices dripped down his chin I slid my body down and he stuck his fingers back inside me and began moving in and out of me making my pussy talk to him with every stroke. Now sitting on his lap he started kissing my neck and sucking and licking on it as my body bounced up and down on his fingers inside of me. Once again I released all my woman hood on him and lay motionless with my face pressed against the walls of the elevator. I jumped up and pulled my panties back on when heard

"Hello? Stand away from the doors and have a seat I'm going to lower the cab and get you out on the fourth floor. Your going to feel a thud but don't worry."

Daddy yelled

"OK"

and smiled at me. Sure enough we felt the elevator move and then a thump although I wasn't so sure how slight it was, and the doors opened. Daddy stood up and wiped his mouth saying nice to meet you. See you tomorrow, and walked out the elevator.

I feel *so* cheep. But cheep feels good. I got a smile on my face that just won't quit. Can't anything mess with me today, nothing? I went through my day at work with not one problem. Everything went smoothly. During my drive home I relived the Elevator over and over. It was so spontaneous. I'm usually a freak but damn wit someone I don't know is a trip.

Chapter 4:

As I walked through my apt door I could smell something cooking. Looking in the kitchen I could see Trae standing at the counter chopping bell peppers.

"Hey honey, how was work?"

Trae said smiling. I laughed and said

"GREAT".

Trae looked at me and said

"hold on bitch you is glowing and shit what happened wit you at work today. Why are you walking in here all teeth?"

Quickly I closed my mouth and turned to walk away. Trae ran over to me and grabbed me by the waist and said

"huh huh where you going? Now I know something is up. Sit your ass down and tell me all the business."

As she pulled me towards the couch I

contemplated if I should tell her or not. But hell I can't keep this one to my self. As I slumped down on the couch I made my body go limp for emphasis. I showed my million dollar smile and closed my eyes. As I did that I could see everything and I could feel everything over and over again. I popped open my eyes so that I wouldn't go on a trip in front of Trae.

"Girl you got to be ready for the stuff that I'm about to tell you. But I got to make sure that you can handle all of this shit that I went through today. Man man man. So I'm on the elevator at work right, and remember I was telling you about the dude I like but could never talk to? Well guess what?"

I could feel myself starting to melt again and I had to try hard to gain my composer.

"Well, we in the elevator and the mother fucker broke down."

Trae gasped and said

"get the fuck out of here".

I couldn't tell if she was being sarcastic or not so I just kept on with my story cause as long as I thought about it I could relive it as well.

"Yes it broke down but that's not all. The only people that were on the elevator at the time were me, and him. ME and HIM. After some lady called down to us to make sure we were OK, he started talking shit like his lap was the best seat in the house. So u know me right? I had to see if he was telling the truth. So I put it in his face and damn't he knew just what to do with it. That shit was so orgasmic. I can't even remember how many times I came within like 20 min. It was amazing. It was fucking great. It felt like joy."

She looked at me and said

"JOY? Alright, damn that sounds like some freaky shit. So this dude work with you?"

I looked at her and said

"naw I don't know where exactly he work at but I know it's in my building."

"Oh so what's mystery mans name?"

I want to say Daddy but instead I just said

"Stacey".

I wondered if he would call me or not.

But shit after what happened in the elevator you would think he would call. I know if he doesn't I'm going to feel extremely cheep. Especially since I'm still going to have to see him every day in the elevator. So now I'm nervous.

"So what you cooking?"

I asked her trying change the subject now.

"Meatloaf, mashed potatoes and gravy and some green beans, it will be ready soon dear. Oh wait I might not be able to call you that much longer huh since you got a man and all."

I shook my head

"kiss my ass; I ain't no man and you will always be my honey dear."

Trae gave me a hug and said

"ok just don't kick me out until I got some where to go."

as I hugged her back I said

"you ain't ever got to go no where".

She walked into the kitchen and began to set the plates for dinner. I got up and walked into my room to freshen up.
By the time I went back into the kitchen Trae had the dinner and wine sitting real pretty on the table. I walked over to the table and sat down. And we ate, laughed and talked for hours. I got up to clear the table and Trae said

"girl, go on in there and lay down I got this. Get some rest and I'll see you in the morning."

Damn I love her. She is truly my best friend. I went back into my room and lay down on the bed. I must have been tired because I was sleep within like five or ten minutes.

At about three O'clock in the morning my cell phone rang. I almost threw it out my window. It was a number I didn't recognize.

"Hello?"

I answered half sleep sounding all groggy and shit.

"Hey sexy it's me Stacey. I couldn't sleep and I wanted to hear your voice. Were you sleeping?"

Now in my mind I'm thinking what the fuck you think its three o'clock in the damn morning, hell yeah I'm sleep. But who was I kidding this was daddy on my phone.

"Yeah but it's cool I'm up now, how are you? Why can't you sleep?"

He kind of made a moaning sound when he said

"well partially because my tongue is hard and I wanted to taste that pretty little kitty of yours again and also cause I thought about you all day and I just wanted to get to know you a little better. So here's what I'm going to do. I'm going to ask you some questions to get to know you and you can just answer them as quickly or as slowly as you want. So the first one is:

"What's your name?"
"Desi"
"Alright Desi, how old are you and what do you do on the sixth floor"
"Well I'm 23 and I'm in customer service in the telemarketing firm"
"Telemarketing huh, that's cool.

Are you wet right now?"
"What you think?"
"Well shit a nigga like me is thinking hell yeah, are you touching it. And if not can you touch it for me?
"Only if you stroke it for me"
"Damn girl I'm already there"

I could hear Stacey moaning on the other end of the phone. And I could feel myself getting wetter with every stroke. As I slid my finger in and out of my cave I noticed that the one finger had become two and slowly two became three. I could feel my walls tighten around my fingers. I could hear Stacey's voice get deeper than all of a sudden go into a slow roar and rumble. I pictured his face. I imagined my hands rubbing his chest and grabbing his back while he shoved his self inside me. At that moment my pussy began to throb. And my own voice began to rumble. My legs began to shake and my hand that was holding the phone to my ear began to squeeze the phone tighter and tighter. Stacey began to whisper into the phone.

"Damn you feel good. You feel so good right now. Ooh you got some good pussy. Let me hear you baby. Make your pussy talk for me."

And it seems like as soon as he said that my fingers began to move in and out faster and faster and they being mixed with my juices began to make my pussy make that talking noise. That slurping sound that only comes when I'm super wet and have already came or am about to come. You know that gushy sound that lets me know that my orgasm is not that far away. As he continued to whisper into the phone in that tone of voice that made my pussy vibrate I could feel myself reaching my climax. Continuing to penetrate myself I closed my eyes and drifted away. My nipples were hard as a rock and with one final whisper of yes I felt myself pour onto my fingers. I felt my leg fall flat and stop shaking to a slow tremble. As I opened my mouth I heard the words damn daddy slip out. Shit did I just say that out load. Oh well it's not like I could take it back.

"No ma I should be saying damn to you. Your pussy is just as good over the phone as it is in person."

That night we talked for hours. Or should I say that morning. He told me everything about him and I did the same. I think I'm in love.

CHAPTER 5:

I'm so sleepy I can't even function right. But I got to get up and get ready for work. I find myself just laying here, drifting back to sleep with thoughts of my elevator passing thru my mind. Yeah I know I said my elevator but after what I did in it to me it would forever be MY elevator.

I jumped in the shower and as the warm water started to beat down my back I could feel my body shiver and tingle. As I brushed my teeth I looked at myself in the mirror. I don't know why but I paid extra attention to how I put my make up on. I swooped my hair in a way that slightly covered my left eye. And I remembered to pick out the perfect outfit. The one that showed my coke bottle frame. No time to eat because I was already running late so I jumped in my car and was ready to start my day. I did not want to be late today and miss my chance to see Daddy in the elevator. Even though we were past the introduction stage I still felt all shy around him. I really wanted to see him again and in a different environment. I wanted to see if he knew how to treat a woman as well as sex one. But I was still unsure as to what I was going to say to him when I finally did see him. I mean should I be the first one to speak or should I wait for him. All these thoughts passed my mind as I pulled into the driveway. My heart began to race and pound and I felt myself get all nervous and anxious

I adjust my skirt and take a quick look in my compact just to make sure my face is straight because I know who walks through the elevator doors on the next floor. He walks in with his smooth creamy chocolate skin, fresh low hair cut edged up nicely with waves that would make you sea sick. As he walks in he grabs me in his arms only for me to realize that his arms don't feel as strong and as he presses my body close against his chest I could feel that daddy has breasts. I push away with a confused look on my face.

"Damn baby what's wrong why up pushing me away like that?"

Stacey asked. I'm speechless and unsure of what to say. My heart is pounding. And Stacey grabs me again and holds me saying

"I thought about you all night or should I say all morning".

As she pulled away I looked in her eyes and still saw the same person I saw a day ago, the same person that I talked to on the phone for hours. The same person that I shared the most spontaneous, passionate experience that I have ever had with. I saw DADDY. As I got ready to exit the

elevator I whispered in her ear I
thought about you too, call me....

www.ingramcontent.com/pod-product-compliance
Lightning Source LLC
Chambersburg PA
CBHW061231280526
45784CB00006B/2725